Introduction to Basic Gin Distillation

By William Bentley

Introduction

Im not writing this to show my knowledge on the history of distillation or the evolution of spirits, or the time line of Gin. This is going to be a bomb proof, bullet proof 101 guide to rectifying spirit through a distillation process to create a quality Gin for the first time.

We will discuss different methods, techniques, botanical relationships, recipe creating and anything I can remember about been curious when I wanted to distill my own Gin for the first time and was not fully sure how.

This is not an advanced guide, or going to be too technical or Scientific, it will be layman terms, basic fundamentals on creating a quality gin, along with analogies to help paint a better picture.

This guide can be applied whether you have a small 1L still or 1500L Alembic Still... the principles are the same.

We will cover the parts of the Still and what each part does, The process of Rectifying spirit, The heads, The hearts and the Tails and Maceration. Then we will look at the botanicals, botanical relationships, flavours and how to apply them to recipes and the distilling process.

I hope you enjoy this read and that it is of use and helps you get started on your Gin making journey.

Good luck and enjoy.

Parts Of The Still

Alembic Still

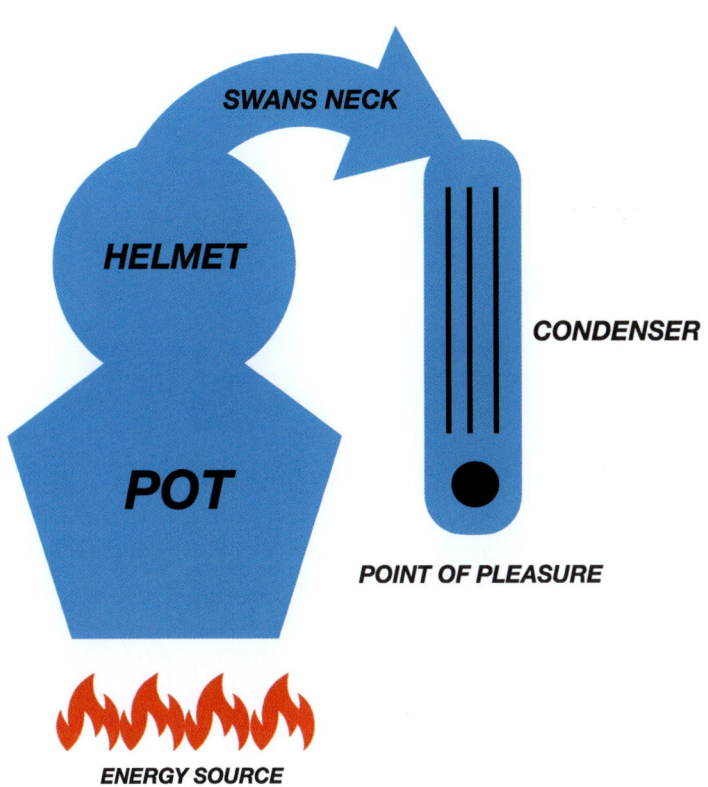

Energy Source:

The Energy/Heat Source can be a variety of types, they all have a different quality, control, efficiency and energy transfer rate. These sources are used to bring your stills "charge" up to heat. You will control this heat source throughout the distillation as different amounts of energy is required for different flavours and notes to pass over the still during the distillation process.

The Pot:

The Pot is at the bottom and is largest Bulbous part of the still, This is where your Charge of Water, Neutral Spirit and Botanicals will sit whilst been heated up to the correct temperatures required.

The Column:

Not all stills have a column, but some do. Some have them separate where the vapour passes through. The idea of this part of the still is so you can have a hanging basket or perforated plate in which you can sit botanicals on. This is to create more delicate and lighter flavour expressions to your gin. Rather than having the ingredients boiling, stewing and mashing around in the hot liquid. This part can either be separate so that the vapour is directed through or it can be located between the pot and the helmet. It will look like an Alembic still but with an elongated neck between the pot and the helmet.

The Helmet:

The helmet is where all the vapour bottle necks and passes over to the swans neck ensuring as much contact with the copper as possible. The more the Vapour *Refluxs* (Condensates) and the longer the Vapour makes conversation with the copper the purer the spirit will be. The Helmet will always take longer to get hot as it is further away from the heat source, but this is a good thing as when your vapour rises from your pot it will keep Refluxing until it reaches a hotter temperature.

The Swans neck:

The Swans neck is called this due to its uncanny appearance, the curvature is designed to start the 1st stage of cooling and descend the vapour down towards the Condenser.

The Condenser:

The condenser is where we pass the Vapour through a spiral of piping. The piping passes through a Sump of continuous flowing chilled water. This is so the vapour will fully condensate back to a liquid.

The Point of Pleasure:

The point of pleasure is where our finished liquid will exit the still at Still Strength. Some stills at this point have a "Parrot Cup" where an ABV (Alcohol By Volume) Hydrometer can sit to keep an eye on the ABV of the liquid flowing through. This can be used as one of many indicators on when to cut your Heads, Hearts and Tails which we will explain later.

Reflux

The shape of the Pot and Helmet are curved and designed to create Reflux; Reflux is when you liquid evaporates to vapour, hits the side of the still and the re-condensates back to a liquid flowing back down to the pot to be Re- Evaporated. We want the still to promote this, as much as possible, the more this happens the more the copper reacts and strips the spirit of its Toxins and Chemicals, and in turn helps purify your spirit.

I like to use the analogy of when the vapour is rubbing against the copper, it is in Conversation, And the longer the conversation it has, the more educated the spirit becomes. The spirit must have multiple Conversations until it is educated enough to graduate and pass over the swans neck, as only a well educated spirit is good enough for the palate.

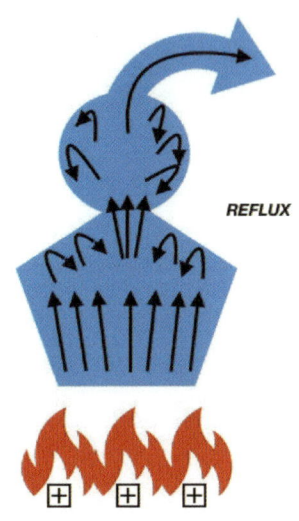

Charging The Still & Maceration

Maceration is leaving your ingredients in the spirit and water for a duration of time and this will all depend on the starting ABV of your Neutral spirit. Whether you are Rectifying 96% grain spirit, or 40% Vodka etc. Your maceration times are up to you, but again it will all depend on your ABV. So the stronger your ABV, the lower your maceration time will be as the high percentage alcohol will rip and strip straight through your botanicals. A lower ABV will obviously take longer but could be a lighter infusion. Also the temperature at which you macerate at will make a huge difference.

Think about a tea bag in cold water or hot water... they will mash at different flavour strengths and for different durations. One could be more bitter and the other sweeter, But all will have a different outcome, different shade and a different flavour profile of tea.

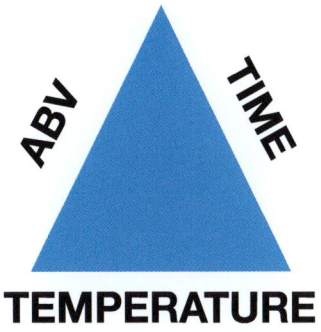

I find a good maceration ABV is around 60-63% ABV for 12-14 hours. Much more than this and you will get a more oily taste and any less you will get lighter or delicate flavour. So use this to your advantage as to what outcome you desire.

You will also want to think about what botanicals you macerate over time and what botanicals you put in the still on the day of the distillation. Maybe any over powering flavours you don't want to macerate, but instead place into the still just before heating up to distill. Maybe your spices need longer than your Citrus, This is up to you as a creator to decide your recipe, maceration times and at what temperature. Some botanicals can turn bitter if macerated for a long duration, some need that time to pull out the flavours. I will discuss botanicals, ratios and recipes further in this book.

The Distillation Process

Before applying heat double check the helmet is sealed to the pot as we do not want any vapour escaping where it shouldn't be. Firstly its dangerous and highly flammable, and also you don't want to waste your produce to the angels. The Only place the vapour should be escaping is through the maze of copper to the condenser to be chilled back to liquid. You secure this seal with either a water and flour paste mix, which will dry and back solid as the still gets hot. Ive also seen used electricians tape or Plumbers PTFE (Plastic tape for engineers) as it seems to be able to with stand the amount of heat that we will be applying.

And also make sure the condenser is flowing with cold water, so that it is ready to condensate the vapour when it passes through.

Now in the pot is a Charge of water, Spirit and botanicals. Water Boils at 100 Degrees Celsius, Where as Alcohols boiling point is 78.3 Degrees Celsius. What we are going to do is separate these 2 mixed liquids by bringing the alcohol to boil without the water reaching its own boiling temperature. Naturally we will get a small percent of bonded water that will pass over through evaporation but don't worry, the art of this is to keep it to a minimum. We should be aiming for our whole distillation to be coming off the still above 70% ABV, Ideally 80%-82%ABV.

We will now add heat/Energy to the pot of the still, We do not want to do this Fast. It is not a rushed process. Think Low and Slow. Slow and steady wins the race. We are going to slowly raise the temperature until our pot reaches 78.3 Degrees Celsius. Once we get there we want to ride between that Temperature and 82 Degrees Celsius. Between this point we will see the helmet temperature rise, which will let our vapour pass over the swans neck and eventually see our first drops of liquid dripping from the point of pleasure. (This will be the beginning of our heads).

Our Condenser cooling liquid Temperature must ideally stay below 30 Degrees Celsius. If we are In the thirties this can equal to a lesser quality liquid and heading towards been unsafe. In the Twenties is a much safer range and any cooler than that is fantastic.

If your still does not have any thermometers I suggest acquiring some and sticking thermometers onto the still, Ideally one for the pot, one for the helmet and one to keep an eye on the condenser temperature. These 3 aids will be rough guidelines and great visual indicators to help you through the process.

Some stills have a viewing window that allows you to monitor how vigorous your charged liquid is behaving. When heating up the pot you will eventually see little sparkles popping on the surface and light mist and the floating botanicals moving slowly side to Side. As we get hotter you will then notice the water looking like its shimmering, as if wind is blowing across steady waters. As the temperature progresses you will get a uniformed ocean like ripples dancing across the surface, until eventually you see a sea of pearls dancing on the surface. This is when the alcohol as reached boiling temperature and is breaking through the surface of the water into vapour.

As a distiller it is up to you to decide where you want to cut the heads, Hearts and Tails. I will explain this in the next Chapter.

Once you have Cut your heads, you will collect your heart section of your distillation. The flavour profile will change through out the overall distillation run. In the beginning you will get your citrus notes and delicate flavours as these don't take as much energy pass over with the vapour. Then mid run your Juniper and piney notes will pass over, then followed by your Heavy Spice notes, which will all make up your final combined flavour profile. The back end of your run may take more energy and heat to get these flavours over the still. So don't worry if you have to drive the temperature a little more at the back end of the distillation run.

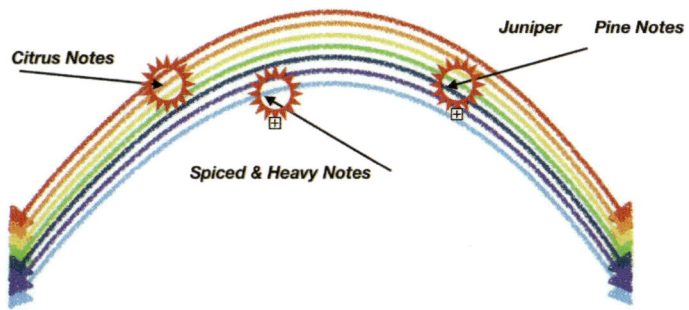

When Distilling the hearts, It is like a Rainbow… in the beginning your sending the delicate flavours over the still with minimum energy, the Reds, Oranges and yellows, These will be predominately Citrus notes. Then mid run we will see the Green and Blues pass over, Which are your Juniper and Piney notes. Then finally you may need to add some more energy to get your darker heavier colours over, the Indigos and Violets. These are normally your Spices, Roots and Barks. These flavours normally help bring a little body to the final Gin.

Eventually you will need to make your cut, as you will be descending into the nutty watery tails region which is starting to lower your overall ABV, Flavour profile and quality. A few Visual tell tale signs will be your Helmet temperature reaching around 86.8 Degrees Celsius, Your ABV Hydrometer in the collecting Parrot Cup / vessel dropping below 80 Degrees

Celsius and heading down towards 70%ABV or less... These are all visual indicators. Though the best tell tale sign you have is your sense of smell and taste. Have a dip, have a taste and train your tongue to know when its not tasting as good as it should. I personally look out for the taste and smell of a watery nutty essence, as remember this is the back end of the hearts run, which is your spices, Barks and Nutty flavours... when that falls weak you need to make your cut to tails to prevent it collecting in the hearts run.

The Heads and Tails Cut is like a pair of goal posts and its up to you how wide or short your goal posts are. The wider the posts, the higher your heart yield is... but the quality is low. The closer your goal posts the lower your heart yield is, but the quality is higher. If the Goal posts are too close to each other you will chop off the beginning and end of your full flavour Spectrum. So you must find a happy balance between, Quality Flavour and yield

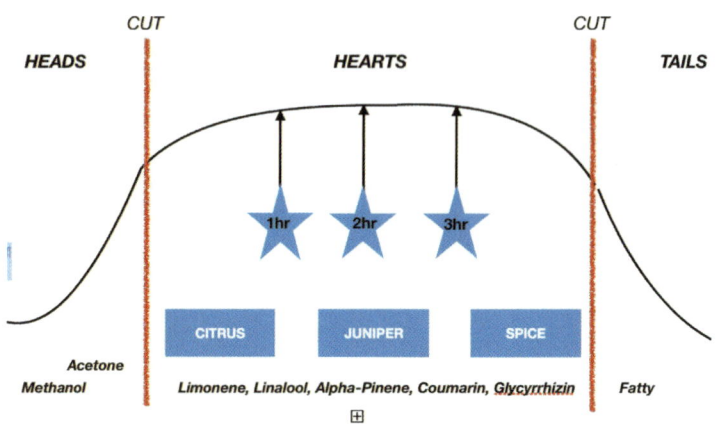

Some recipes may have a different Cut ratios depending on what botanicals are in the recipe, what altitude your distilling at etc. But as a Distiller this is your judgement, your taste and your preference.

Heads, Hearts And Tails

I find that the heads bears a similar character to that of a cheap aftershave methanol smell and taste, or cleaning product. When this fades out and I can then start to notice the citrus notes coming through, its as if the flavour almost becomes technicolor. This is your turning point from Heads to Hearts. If you are unsure in the beginning make several cuts in separate collecting vessels, this way you can taste and smell each one and decide for yourself, as you will notice a big difference amidst each sample. You can also apply this technique to your tails cut, and once you decide where your final cut is going to be, you can discard the waste and mix back in the good samples.

A good safe and Premium style of Cut to ensure No chemicals fall over into your hearts is as loosely as follows: *(But remember to trust your tastebuds)*

Working out From your Charge of Grain Spirit @ 96% (Ignoring the water addition as a lot of this will remain in the still at the end of your distillation, remember your separating the alcohol, so this maths applies to the alcohol content only)

2% Heads

80-82% Hearts

16-20% Tails

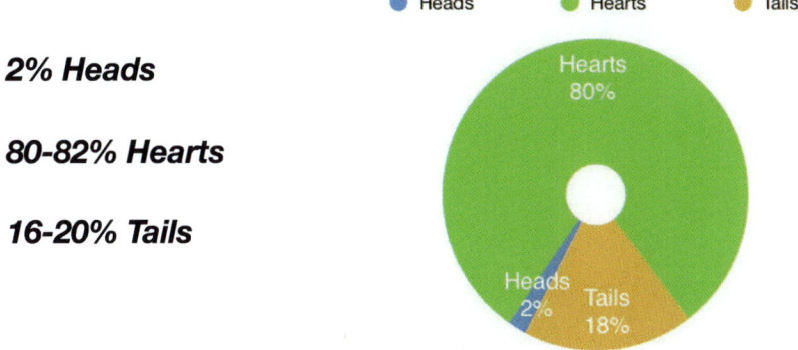

Remember these examples are guidelines and the cuts may move each way ever so slightly depending on botanicals, desired result, quality and yield

Example 1:

30L of Grain Spirit @ 96% would equal:

2% of 30L = 600ml Heads

80% of 30L = 24L Hearts

18% of 30L = 5.4L Tails

The above charges would obviously have an additional 16-18L water added to bring down the 96% Neutral spirit to around 60% ABV for maceration and safety, But do your maths and work out from the charge of alcohol content. This is for the reason of their is no heads and tails in water. The chemicals we are removing is in the Neutral spirit, So this equation is for quantity of Spirit not water.

Example 2:

If you were to Distill 1L of 40% Vodka, that would mean 40% of that litre is pure alcohol. So the above equation would be working with 400ml of alcohol (40%)

2% of 400ml = 8ml Heads

80% of 400ml = 320ml Hearts

18% of 400ml = 72ml Tails

The Above then adds back up to 400ml of alcohol, as 600ml of that bottle of vodka you are re distilling is 60% Water. Once you have collected your 72ml of tails you are practically turning water into vapour and collecting water and waste produce (No more alcohol). This is then your by product (Wash), Spent botanicals and waste.

Types of Distillation

One Shot:

One shot distillation is when the still is loaded with the right amount of botanicals and spirit to make the required amount of Gin once watered down. IE; once the Charge is distilled and ready to be bottled, the only thing added is water to make it bottling strength. The downside to this is you can only make what you put in the still and as demand grows you will need more stills or production time. The plus side is you are making small batch, hand crafted Gin and ensuring quality at every stage

Concentrate:

Concentrate distillation is when the botanical content is multiplied and dialled up to make more bottles of gin. Let me explain; Essentially you could put 10-1000x the amount of botanicals in the still, and once distilled it would be treat as a concentrate. So before bottling or watering down to bottle strength a neutral grain spirit will be added to bulk and stretch out the concentrate. Just like a cordial or fruit concentrate drink. The downside to this method is that your adding neutral spirit that has not gone through your distillation process and will still contain the chemicals and toxins you normally remove with the heads and tails cut. Also working out how far to stretch the concentrate can alter your original or desired flavour profile. The plus side is you can create more bottles off one run. The big debate is whether or not this loses quality through mass production. Though many brands including major labels do this to keep up with the market demand.

Distillates:

Another method is to distill each botanical separately and create a library of individual flavoured distillates and then proceed to blend your own gin recipe, some believe you have more options and control over your flavours this way. You can swap and tweak as you please. It also enables you to then just make one bottle at a time of whatever recipe you want and keep the process very bespoke. This is almost a hybrid of the 2 other approaches because each flavour distillate will be one shot. Or you can make a concentrate of each flavour, so you just need a drop of a few desired flavours to make your base concentrate and then top up with neutral spirit and water.

The one shot method and concentrate method has been an ongoing argument over quality and necessity, Some say you cant taste the difference… but does that mean its ok? Some say that if your neutral spirit is top quality it shouldn't have much toxins and chemicals in it to begin with, so concentrate is fine. Some of the top shelf brands use the concentrate method but we just never knew about it. This is totally up to you as a distiller to what you think is right and necessary for what you want to achieve.

Another on going argument is whether Copper is any better or superior to other metal or glass made stills… Copper is undoubtedly a fantastic conductor of heat and energy and is a metal that oxidises and reacts against other elements, but some believe it doesn't make a difference in distillation. Call me old fashioned or a puritan but I believe copper and the one shot method is the method for me.

Copper stills are all about taste. When distilling, the copper reacts on a molecular level with compounds containing sulphur that are produced by yeast during the early fermentation stages of your base spirit. The product of this reaction is copper sulphate which remains in the still, rather than in the distillate, thus allowing the organic compounds that give recognisable aromatic aromas to shine through in the finished spirit.

Botanicals, Recipes and Ratios

Most Gins are built around what we call the **Famous 4:**

Juniper

Coriander

Orris Root

Angelica Root

If this was music then these would be your notes that make up a major chord. If these were colours in an artists palette, then these would be their primary colours.

Not all Botanicals are in a Gin for their flavours, Some are in there to support other flavours or to imitate another flavour. You may not taste them, but you would lack taste without them. Like you never taste Salt in a soup, yet its in there to enhance the tomato and it would lack without it. It is also good to remember that some flavours once distilled don't tase how you imagine them to taste. Distilling can sometimes change the flavour profile *(not all the time, but sometimes)*.

So Legally by Law, **Juniper** must be Predominant, Not always as a quantity, could be as a taste or a smell, it must be predominant to be legally a London Dry Gin. Juniper gives that Classic Piney taste we know so well in Gin. The amount of Juniper that goes into the making of 1 bottle of Gin may surprise you… its nothing more than 4-10 tiny berries.

Coriander is a Seed and a Spice. Within distillation coriander brings citrus notes to the flavour profile, not spice. There is some big brand Gins on the market that has no citrus in the recipe but on the pallet you get citrus notes.

Orris Root gives a floral, perfume, sweet Palma violet taste when distilled and works as a binding agent to help hold all the flavours and smells together

Angelica root is also a binding botanical, with its earthy taste it also helps hold together the body of flavours and longevity of flavour when in the mix.

I find Orris Binds the smells of botanical notes together and creates a longevity on the nose, whereas Angelica does the same for the tasting notes, body and flavour.

If these Famous 4 Botanicals were The Beatles then the 5th Beatle would be Liquorice Root. This botanical not only brings sweetness to a Gin when distilled, a large amount in the mix can also Bring Dryness to the pallet after been sipped, Which can be great for a gin that is aimed for a dry martini. Finding the turning point and balance between sweet and dry is the complicated part of balancing this botanical.

The 3 Classic Citrus Peels are Lemon, Bitter orange and Grapefruit. Generally these work best dried, but also fresh peels can bring a crispness zest life to a gin.

In the Spice section your obvious classics are Cinnamon, Cassia Bark, Cardamom, Nutmeg, Pepper and Almond. These bring the body and heavier notes to the flavour profile, so be careful of how much of these you may want to add. These are big robust flavours all fighting for a place within the spectrum of your gin.

Classic London Dry gins tend to be between 4-10 Ingredients, 12 at a push. Your more artisanal flavour gins can have up to 47 and more. Remember the more you put in, the more space, support and relationships each flavour is fighting for.

Ratios And Guidelines Regarding Botanicals

With your recipes you must decide what sort of Gin you are trying to create and to what purpose will this Gin be used for and work backwards to reverse engineer that process to your raw ingredients. Do you want a classic Robust London dry that Cuts through well in a gin and Tonic but can stand the beating of been stirred down in a martini, or are you looking to make something a little quirky and off the wall. Or Maybe you want a heavily spiced Gin that concentrates more on the heavy spice notes. As a distiller this is what you need to decide, and with my Recipe guidelines, you should be able to guide yourself in the right direction to create some basic and solid recipes. Remember these are just a starting reference point, and I highly recommend tweaking, going off piste and doing your own thing. But as a starting point I hope the below information helps.

FAMOUS 4:

Juniper 40%

Coriander 10%

Orris Root 3%

Angelica Root 3%

FAMOUS 5:

Juniper 40%

Coriander 10%

Orris Root 3%

Angelica Root 3%

Liquorice 3%

(If you are to dial up any of the above flavours, start to do so in 3% increments)

Powerful long lasting flavours:

(For example: Cardamom, Fennel, Pepper, Star Anise, Cloves etc)

1% - 2%

BASIC FLAVOUR CATEGORIES

DRY: *Teas, Liquorice, Gentian Root, Ginseng, Bergamot*

LONG LASTING SPICE: *Pink pepper, Black Pepper, White Pepper, Cassia Bark, Nutmeg, Fennel, Star Anise, Cinnamon, Clove*

CITRUS: *Bitter Orange, Lemon, Grapefruit, Pomello, Lime, Apple, Quince*

CLASSICS: *Cardamom, Coriander, Nutmeg*

FLORAL: *Rose, Jasmine, Orange Blossom, Petals, Lemongrass, Kaffe Leaf, Hibiscus*

HERBACEOUS: *Dil, Sorrel, Monks Beard, Basil, Chervil, Coriander leaf, Thyme, Mint, Sage, Juniper, Rosemerry, Bay Leaf*

When I personally start developing a new Gin, My default starting ratio for a 1 bottle run would be built firstly upon:

Juniper: 5g

Coriander: 3g

Angelica: 1g

Orris: 1g

(Additional Complimenting Spices less than a gram. Featured flavours obviously amplify)

Then depending on what other flavours I'm adding will determine what I dial up or draw back in the recipe. If I'm going fruity I would raise that juniper and dial up the fruit flavours, If I was heading in a Citrus direction I would instead dial up the coriander. If I was going for floral then I would look at tweaking my Orris up, as the orris has very much a Palma Violet floral notes when heavy in the recipe which may lend towards Rose, Petals or anything in the floral category. If I'm heading in a Spice direction I would look at tweaking my Angelica as I find this brings good savoury earthy notes as a bed for my additional spice flavours to sit upon.

Some botanicals can help bring body to a Gin, Such as Almond, nutmeg, Black Cardamom and Green Cardamom. In my experience these heavier notes come over at the back end of the distillation and bring Bass notes to the final flavour. They really help round up the bottom end of the flavour spectrum, you may have to hold back your tails cut to capture some the heavier notes.

I find Almond brings a Creamy expression to the final liquid, where as Black cardamom brings a smoky rich body with spiced chocolate notes, Pairs well with Coffee and other dark heavy flavours.

When dealing with over powering flavours and spices, we need to look at really dialling these down in the recipe as you will be surprised how potent of a flavour they are.

I like to approach it like a golf swing, its not how hard and powerful you hit the ball, its about hitting it right with the perfect swing. Technique over power will send that ball just as far! Just a tiny pinch of pink pepper or star anise sat right in a recipe will shine and cut through in the final flavour.

This applies to overpowering flavours such as:

Star Anise, Pink Pepper, Green Cardamom, Fennel, Bay Leaf, Cumin, Caraway etc.

BUILDING A RECIPE

(THE THOUGHT PROCESS)

When thinking of flavours its great to look at the culinary world and how food is paired and matched in recipes from around the globe and apply this to your Gin recipe building. You will have a main flavour you maybe want to shine, then look at the relationship of that flavour to other flavours in cooking and drinks, and use them other flavours to compliment.

For Example Tomato Soup. Tomato is the Front flavour of the soup, its named after it, Its the leading role. But then lets look at its supporting actors and actresses, You have onion, Pepper, Salt, Basil, Garlic etc. Without these surrounding flavours, the tomato soup is pretty much boring, flat and flavourless.

So lets say I'm going to make a Gin that has a Coffee Expression, Id look around the globe and see cuisines and drink pairings that historically work well with Coffee.

- **Banoffee Pie (Coffee, Toffee and Banana)**

- **Affogato (Coffee and Vanilla Ice cream)**

- **Coffee and Coriander (Moroccan Coffee Serve)**

- Coffee and Cardamon (Arabic Coffee Serve)

- Cardamon & Banana (Raita Sauce for Indian Curry)

- Banana and cinnamon (Flambe banana dessert)

- Coffee and Cinnamon (Mexican Coffee Serve)

- Banana and Anise (Tiramisu & Liquorice Ice cream)

- Anise and Almond (Biscotti)

- Banana and Almond (Banana Split Dessert)

- Cinnamon and Orange (Mulled wine/Christmas pairing)

So from a quick brainstorming session of how flavours correlate together in the culinary world, We can now pull together a pool of ingredients to start tweaking and working into a recipe, We can also see how these ingredients pair well with classic gin ingredients. We could even start branching out from these pairings to see what else the pairings will pair with, but lets not run before we can walk. So lets pool these ingredients:

Juniper, Coffee, Banana, Vanilla, Coriander Seed, Cardamom, Cinnamon, Orange Peel, star anise, Liquorice, Almond.

So from this we have Fruit, Pine, Spice, nut and citrus. Which is starting to look like a good body of botanicals for a gin recipe. A good spider Diagram works well too, That way you can start linking flavours from already linked flavours, and sometimes you see 2nd and and 3rd flavours bridging to each other around your main flavour of choice.

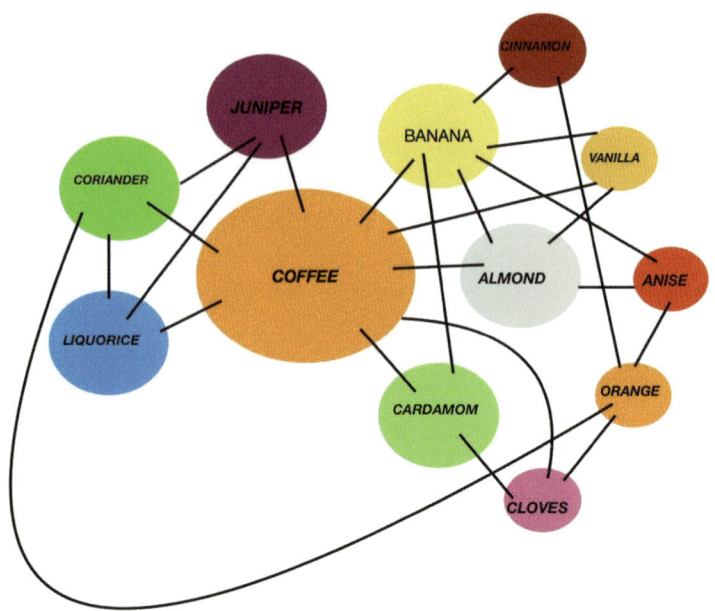

Now if you work loosely with the ratios I mentioned previously in this book, you can hopefully now start to put a recipe together for a first distillation run. Obviously you should be looking at finding what flavours suite you and what you want to achieve, then do a similar brainstorming session.

Another thing to keep in mind is to look at dehydrating certain botanicals. I personally find this works best with citrus, Berries and fruit, anything with a juice or high water content. As when dehydrating the citrus you are removing its water content and concentrating the flavours and its oils. So naturally a gram of Dried Peels would be more concentrated in flavour than a Gram of fresh Peels. But then again maybe you want that delicate taste that only fresh Peels can bring to the table. Or maybe a balance of both? As a distiller this is for you to decide.

INDUSTRY REFERENCE

As an industry reference lets look at some top gin brands and see what botanicals they use, Have a look at what we have discussed regarding flavour relationships and see if you can spot and connections between different botanicals, or try understand why they are in the recipe, and what each botanical brings to the table within that gin, and what the gin is known for:

Tanqueray:

43.1% Export Strength

Juniper, Angelica Root, Coriander Seed, Liquorice Root.

Hendricks:

41.4%

Juniper, coriander, angelica root, orris root, orange peel, lemon peel, cubeb berries, grains of paradise, caraway seeds, elderflower, yarrow and chamomile, Cucumber essence, Rose petal Essence.

Gordons:

37.5%

Juniper, Lemon Peel, Orange Peel (Bitter), Angelica Root, Coriander Seed, Orris Root, Liquorice Root,

Beefeater:

40%

Juniper, Lemon Peel, Orange Peel (Bitter), Angelice root, Coriander Seed, Orris root, Liquorice Root, Cinnamon, Cassia Bark,

Sipsmith:

41.6%

Juniper, Lemon Peel, Orange Peel (Bitter), Angelica Root, Coriander Seed, Orris Root, Liquorice Root, Cinnamon, Cassia Bark, Ground Almond.

Bombay Sapphire:

40%

Juniper, Lemon Peel, Angelica Root, Coriander Seed, Orris Root, Liquorice Root, Cinnamon, Ground Almond.

Boodles:

40%

Juniper, Angelica Root, Angelica Seed, Coriander Seed, Cassia Bark, Nutmeg, Caraway, Rosemary, Sage.

Pickerings:

42%

Juniper, Lemon Peel, Lime Peel, Angelica Root, Coriander Seed, Anise, Cardamom, Cloves, Sage.

Bathtub:

43.3%

Juniper, Orange Peel, Coriander Seed, Cinnamon, Cardamom, Cloves.

Botanist:

46%

Juniper, Lemon Peel, Orange Peel (Bitter), Angelica Root, Coriander Seed, Orris Root, Liquorice Root, Cinnamon, Cassia Bark, Apple Mint, Birch Leaves, Bog Myrtle Leaves, Chamomile (Sweet), Creeping Thistle Flowers, Elderflowers, Gorse Flowers, Heather Flowers, Hawthorn Flowers, Juniper (Prostrate) Berries, Lady's Bedstraw flowers, Lemon Balm, Meadow Sweet, Peppermint Leaves, Mugwort Leaves, Red Clover Flowers, Sweet Cicely Leaves, Tansy, Thyme Leaves, Water Mint Leaves, White Clover, Wood Sage Leaves.

Portobello 171:

42%

Juniper, Coriander Seed, Angelica Root, Orris Root, Lemon Peel, Orange Peel, Liquorice Root, Cassia Bark, Nutmeg.

Bulldog:

40%

Juniper. Coriander Seed, Angelica Root, Cassia Bark, Lemon Peel, Almond, Lotus Leaves, Dragon Eye, Poppy Seed, Lavender, Liquorice Root, Orris Root.

Herno:

40.5%

Juniper, Coriander Seed, Lemon Peel, Vanilla, Black Peppercorns, Lingdon Berries, Cassia Bark, Meadowsweet.

Bottling Strength

When choosing your bottling strength for your new Gin, there is a few things to consider. You cant use normal tap water, you must used Distilled (De-mineralised water), this is to prevent your Gin going cloudy or milky coloured. This is a reaction between the alcohol and non soluble minerals within normal water.

The second thing to consider is your ABV. Remember It has to be at least 37.5% or above to be a Gin.

Like every song has its perfect tempo where the Rhythm and melodies really hit home, every spirit has its its perfect ABV where the botanicals really shine and cut through at their best.

Each recipe will have its own ABV depending on what botanicals and ratios are in there, The best bet is to take a few samples and try taste them at different ABV's, you want enough water in there to dampen the flavour of alcohol to let the botanical flavours shine through, but not too much that you lose the body and bite behind the flavours. Remember its all about balance right through from your recipe up until reducing to bottle strength.

Checking the ABV

For this task you will need your self some Alcohol / Spirit Hydrometers, a good measuring trial jar and a thermometer. Also a Practical Alcohol Tables book to cross reference your results (For all the above a good starting point is Stevenson Reeves)

You will take the Temperature of the liquid and then using your hydrometer measures the specific gravity (Relative density) of liquids: The ratio of the density of the liquid to the density of water. Using the scale on the hydrometer to read the specific gravity

With the temperature and the specific Gravity reading, you will cross reference these using your book of Practical Alcohol Tables to find the actual ABV of the liquid. You can then use this formula below to work out how much water is needed to bring down to your desired bottling strength.

Desired ABV Calculator Formula

This formula is for you to work out your bottling strength, if you struggle, there is websites online that you can input your information into and select your desired ABV and it will do the maths for you.

$$\frac{ABV1 \times VOL1}{ABV2} = VOL2$$

$$VOL2 - VOL1 = \triangle ADD$$

Your Current ABV (Times) The Current Quantity of Liquid.

(Divide) that by your Desired ABV = Y

Then take Y (Minus) your Original Quantity of Liquid.

The answer is then the amount of Demineralised water you need to add to reach your final desired ABV

Types, Styles & Categories Of Gin

There is different categories and styles of gin, Some our bound by legalities or geographical locations to be defined as a certain style and some not.

The EU Gin Definition is as follows:

All gins are made with ethyl alcohol alcohol flavoured with juniper berries (juniperus communis) and other flavourings. The ethyl alcohol used must be distilled to the minimum standards stated in the EU Spirit Drink Regulations. In all types of gin, the predominant flavour of must be juniper, and they must have a minimum retail strength of 37.5% abv. There are three definitions of gin: gin, distilled gin and London Gin.

London Dry:

London Dry Gin is made in a traditional still by re-distilling ethyl alcohol (Neutral Spirit) in the presence of all natural flavourings used.

- The ethyl alcohol used to distil London Dry Gin must be of a higher quality than the standard laid down for ethyl alcohol.

The methanol level in the ethyl alcohol must not exceed a maximum of 5 grams per hectolitre of 100% vol. alcohol.

- The flavourings used must all be approved natural flavourings and they must impart the flavour during the distillation process.

- The use of artificial flavourings is not permitted.

- The Final distillate at still strength must have a minimum strength of 70% abv.

- No flavourings can be added after distillation.

- Further ethyl alcohol may be added after distillation provided it is of the same standard.

- A small amount of sweetening may be added after distillation provided the sugars do not exceed 0.1 grams/litre of finished product (the sugar is not discernible and is added to some products purely for brand protection purposes).

- The only other substance that may be added is water.

- London Gin cannot be coloured.

Distilled Gin:

Distilled gin is made in a traditional still by:

- Redistilling neutral alcohol in the presence of natural flavourings.

- There is no minimum strength laid down for the resultant distillate.

- After distillation, further ethyl alcohol of the same composition may be added.

- Additional flavourings may be added after distillation and these can be either natural or artificial flavourings.

- The distillate can be further changed by the addition of other approved additives since there is no prohibition on their use in the definition.

- Water may be added to reduce the strength to the desired retail level.

- There is no restriction on the colouring of distilled gin with approved colourings.

Plymouth:

Plymouth Gin is a Protected by its Geographical location and states that Plymouth gin must be distilled in Plymouth. Plymouth gin is also watered down using Dartmoor water.

Genever Or Dutch Gin:

Genever is a predecessor to the style of gin that we know as London Dry Gin. Traditionally the base of Genever had a high percentage of Malt Wine (15%-50%), resulting in a spirit that had similar weight on the palate and malty notes like whiskey, and a herbal component that is common with gin. It is also can be barrel aged.

Old Tom Gin:

Old Tom Gin (or Tom Gin or Old Tom) is a gin recipe popular in 17th-18th-century England. It is slightly sweeter than London Dry, but slightly drier than the Dutch Genever, thus is sometimes called "the missing link"

Sloe Gin:

A liqueur made by steeping sloes in gin and including the addition of Sugar. Generally a dark cherry red colour. Sloe berries are a stoned fruit from the plum family.

Things To Note And Things you Don't

- Turning up the heat to speed up the distillation run will only result in a lower ABV as more water will pass over the still, and also unwanted heavy compounds (IE: you will be sending over your tails/Fatty Acids sooner than needed or wanted).

- Only every fill the still to 80% of its capacity, So for example a 10L Still will hold 8L of Charge

- Do not over fill your still as when the liquid bubbles and boils it could send over your maceration liquid which will entail in non distilled liquid coming over. You know this if your collecting liquid is discoloured or murky.

- From the stills pot to collecting the spirit, there should be no blockages in the process as this can result in a pressure build up and eventually exploding

- Make sure all parts of the Still and sealed properly to prevent Vapour leakage as this is dangerous and highly flammable, Keep well ventilated and take the upmost care

- Never allow the still to boil dry as the heat will not be able to transfer passed the copper and could buckle or deform your still and joints may Separate. And on the flip side be careful not to flash cool you still when done.

- Cool the still or let it cool before opening

- Never Fill alcohol into a hot still, always start from Cold.

- Make sure your Condenser water is cool enough to promote the vapour to condense, if not you will have a vapour cloud exiting your still and as mentioned before its dangerous and highly flammable

- Do not try distilling 96% Neutral grain spirit, you must add water and bring down the ABV, to make it less volatile and less dangerous. (You have seen what happens when pouring wine or spirit onto a hot pan when cooking, It will Auto ignite. The same could happen within the still.

- Always wash and clean your still in-between distillations, whether its a good rinse with water, or a deeper clean with Caustic soda and then citric acid. Either way rinse thoroughly with water.

- If you spill high percentage alcohol then you should be watering it down quickly with at least the same amount of water to reduce risk of it been flammable, then cleaned accordingly.

- By all means get familiar with your heads and tails. The smell and the taste, to help educate and train your palette and sense of smell. But don't consume or drink any sizeable quantities, we cut these parts out for a reason!

- Good spirits warm on the inside, bad spirits burn on the way down. You should be aiming for a smooth Gin that isn't rough or burns, and is acceptable to sip neat without burning. That is a sure fire sign of a well balanced recipe, correctly cut and well distilled Gin.

Epilogue:

I hope this literature has served a purpose and got you started in the production of your own Gin making journey. I wrote this book to answer all the questions I couldn't find the answers for in the beginning. This should get you footed with a basic understanding in the practical side of distilling, so you can get the ball rolling and then the science and heavier knowledge will naturally follow as your curiosities unravel further.

Play safe and Enjoy

William Bentley.